OUR
DINOSAURS
ARE DYING

by
Kenan
Heise

NEW AMERICAN POETRY

ISBN: 0-924772-26-3

10 9 8 7 6 5 4 3 2 1

To Evelyn, my mother,
who went away on her ship.

To Carol, my wife and friend,
and to Paully, my big brother,
who encouraged me.

Introduction

Poems, meet my friend, the reader.
Good reader, meet my friends, these poems.

∼ K.H.

Special Thanks

*To Gwendolyn Brooks
and Bob Greene,
who have given
this book of poems
their high fives.*

Our Dinosaurs are Dying

Across America,
where once rollercoasters roared
down and up
rickety ladders of wood,
now stand
shopping malls,
subdivisions
and fast food restaurants.
Although a comet didn't cause it,
our dinosaurs are dying.

US

A City Person

I am a city person.
We don't count
traffic lights
to give directions
and we know where
at least
a dozen restaurants are.
I am a sophisticated urban resident.
We know what a queue is
and have stood
in lots of them.
We have different rules.
We do not visit folks
where they work.
To us,

       a garage,

       a store,

       or an office

is not a social place.
We do not know
the name of the manager
of our

       local supermarket,

       drugstore,

       bakery,

       theater

       or gas station.

We don't have to walk
down by the road
a bit

to collect our mail.
Most of us
did not go
to our local high school
and neither will
our grandchildren.
Our parents
and ancestors
are not buried
on a hill
along the highway.
We don't know the name
of the family that lives
in the really big house on the hill
and we are not distantly related to them.
We do not get to read in our local papers
about who has been out of town
visiting relatives.
I am city person.
We don't see many stars
at night
and can get very excited
if we recognize the Big Dipper.
What is an ice cream social?

Whence, Whither, Why?

Whence,
whither,
why?
As we move around
the oval track of life,
I think I hear
someone laughing.
I wonder:
Is there a grandstand?

The AIDS Quilt

Ask not for whom
the quilt is sewn.
It is stitched for your friend,
the one who died from AIDS.
You had no such friend,
you say?
Who is your friend
if not he and she
who cared,

    created,

    taught,

    acted,

    played piano,

    made movies,

    sold antiques,

    researched medicine,

    took pictures,

    authored books,

    reported news,

    soldiered,

    said mass,

    ministered,

    drove cabs or buses,

    collected garbage,

    assembled cars,

    organized,

    waitressed or waitered,

    repaired phones,

    delivered mail?

All these things
and many, many more
did the names on the quilt
do for others and for you.
Some of them,
mere children,
only suffered and died for us.
Call them friends
and ask them not
for whom the quilt is sewn.
It is stitched
for you and me
to tell us our friends are dying.

The New American Poets

I hear America poetic.
We all do.
It is the voice
        of newness,
                originality,
                direct, eloquent language,
                fresh thoughts
        and strong ideas.
It is poetry
offered,
for a suddenly-receptive America,
        in coffeehouses,
        on the campus,
        by letter,
        in bookstores,
        over the fence,
        though magazines,
        in books,
        at gatherings,
        on dates,
        through poetry organizations,
        over the radio
        and on MTV.
This poetry
        inaugurated the Clinton presidency,
                waking up the sleepers
                with excitement
                and finely tuned thought and expression.

It is words,
>>rhythm,
>>thought,
>>reflection,
>>experience,
>>emotion,
>>truth,
>>hope
>>and promise.
But, it can also be
>>cacophony,
>>despair,
>>fear,
>>anger,
>>bitterness,
>>frustration,
>>cynicism
>>and hurt.
It is very human,
felt from the gut, the heart and the head,
this new poetry,
uttered
with cracking,
determined,
teeth-clinched speech;
but also stated just as often
>>softly,
>>earnestly,
>>gently,
>>fervently,

OUR DINOSAURS ARE DYING

with beauty rather than anger,
with thought more than emotion,
with mirth rather than laughter.
It is

>   historic and visionary,
>   relative and prophetic,
>   agnostic and religious,
>   subatomic and cosmic,
>   placid and explosive,
>   hell-driven and heaven-bent.

The new poetry

>   is flowered words,
>   visceral protest,
>   explicit romance,
>   and elaborate dream castles.

It is we
on a spree,
being ourselves
and trying to express that.
Amen and hallelujah
to the new American poets,
one and all!

Hey!

"Hey!"
he yelled.
That's "Hello"
in a lot of places
in this country.
It's usually
a friendly greeting,
a right congenial one.
The rest of us,
when we were kids,
if we used the word,
people would say,
"Hay's for horses"
or
"Straw is cheaper."
Personally,
I don't know why
or whether or nay,
straw is cheaper
than hay.

The Big "What If?"

What would have happened
had a noble Roman
waged a successful campaign
against the death penalty
throughout the empire
in say, 30 A.D.?
What a wonderful,
pagan thing
that would have been!

Door to Door in the Depression

It was the Depression
and he was a boy
selling flowers
door to door.
He went
to the neighborhood
where they had all the money.
"Aren't these flowers pretty?"
he asked.
"Only 5 cents a piece,"
he added hopefully;
but they didn't buy any.
He went to the poor neighborhood,
where they had
more troubles than money.
"Aren't these flowers pretty?"
he asked.
"Very much so,"
they said.
"Only 5 cents a piece,"
he added.
"If I can find a nickel,"
they answered.
And usually
they did.

Waiting for Her Ship to Come In

While things did get better,
their ship never did come in.

It was dreamed about,
but it didn't reach shore.

It was an actual ship,
of course.
She heard
the big people, the adults,
talk about it.
That's how she knew
it was a real one.

"When our ship comes in,"
she heard them say.
They smiled down at her
when she asked about it.
She'd have a new dress
when their ship came in.

That was a specific promise
from Momma.

Poppa added,
"Ice cream every Sunday afternoon."
She had her own, secret list,
for when their ship came it.

A bed of her own,
not with her two sisters.

A bedroom of her own,
but she scratched that off her list
for when their ship came in,
but a new doll was there
and a trip to the city

and a ride on the streetcar.
　　　　A box of candies,
with only soft centers
when their ship came in.
　　　　And nice things
for Poppa and Momma
and even for her sisters
if they treated her nice
before their ship came in.
Ninety years have passed
and the ship didn't come in.
Things got better.
Momma and Poppa left.
Did they go away on ships?
No. They died,
but it was like they had.
She met a man, married him,
loved him for 40 years
and he died, sailed off.
Her oldest son, gone too.
But their ship never came in.
Or did it?
One did come,
does come,
bringing memories
rather than gold
and they're much better
than ice cream,
every Sunday afternoon.

Father's Day

Happy Father's Day,
Dad!
So, who says
your ten year old
isn't the right person
to pick out a tie
or that you didn't really need
one more sports shirt?
So what
if your teenager
had to be reminded
or your college student deduction
forgot?
Who do you think you are,
their mother?
The phone company
gives us the facts:
23 million more calls
were logged on Mother's Day,
but collect calls
ran 27% higher
on this day honoring you.

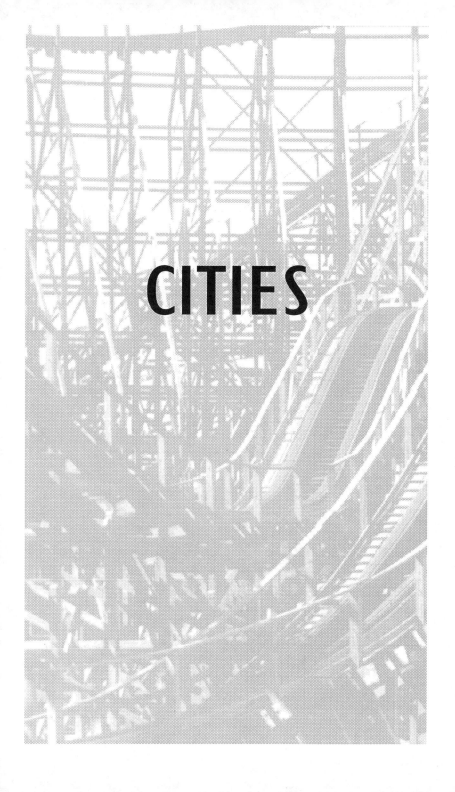

CITIES

Sensing the City

I am old
for I remember
"Rags, old iron,"
yelled down the alleys of the city.
I can recall "Extra"
hollered on streetcorners,
the clang of a streetcar,
the "ooga, ooga" of an unrestored Model T,
the roar of coal down a chute,
the neighing of a milk wagon horse,
the "hooot" of a factory whistle
and the "whrrr" of a scissor sharpener's wheel.
I treasure these sounds, now faint,
as I do the smell
of ice and canvass
on back of the ice wagon
and the taste
of the cream that popped up
out of frozen milk bottles.
These are treasures
of my childhood.
I fantasize
that someday
I'll experience them again
and be young
once more.

I ❤ NY

I love New York,
I really do.
 That big, big city
is like an older brother
to me,
one who's been
  in jail,
  around the world
  and married three times.
For what he does,
he has reasons.
Maybe, his attitude
is because of
                a dark night
                going around the Horn
                or having fought off
                a sadistic guard
                in maximum security.
New York
                can sing,
                can write,
                can act
and likes to drink;
no, has to drink.
And he can love,
but, it's not his first impulse.
I love New York,
                but I have seen
                one of its cops

kicking a man
in Times Square
because the man was drunk,
sprawled on the sidewalk,
unconscious.
I love New York,
but I've been
propositioned there
while walking down the street
with my wife.
I love New York,
but I've seen
its sweatshop slaves
at rows of sewing machines
behind closed windows
in the Garment District.
I love New York,
but I've witnessed
its drug pushing
in the Village.
I love New York,
but I've been confused
by its pace
and scared
by its brutality and violence,
the sickening kind
you feel part of
when it's an older brother
in a fitful rampage.

OUR DINOSAURS ARE DYING

I love New York,
>   because I have viewed
>   the now-you-know-everything
>   documentaries
>   on the Brooklyn Bridge
>   and the Statue of Liberty;
>   because I've seen the movies
>   that romanticized the city
>   and the ones that junked it;
>   because I've heard its accents
>   and polyglot tongues;
>   because there are enclaves there
>   called boroughs
>   and subways that,
>   in a million years,
>   a visitor could not fathom
>   nor want to.

I love New York,
>   because the blood
>   that pulsates there
>   is as mine.

I too love
>   to accomplish,
>   to experience,
>   to escape boredom,
>   to succeed,
>   to know,
>   to feel
>   and to be as human
>   as I can be.

But, I've never
        been to jail,
        around the world,
        married three times
and there never has been
        a dark night going around the Horn
        or spent fighting a sadistic guard
        in maximum security.

Trains

Trains.
Have you ever noticed
they go away
but their magic doesn't?

Staged in Los Angeles

H-O-L-L-Y-W-O-O-D,
letters on a fault.
atop a hill
outside of
the City of Angels.
They could come tumbling down,
that's for sure,
and be an earthquake sound bite
for the network news.
The people
in and around
Los Angeles
are certain,
however,
that the worst happens
only in movies
and that,
even then,
the goods guys survive.
So they perch
their homes
on the sides of hills
from which
they could slide down.
For generations,
they defied the ocean
with a long, wooden pier.
They build superhighways

that move the cars,
but leave the pollution.
Those people in L.A.
are confident characters
who know
all the world's a stage
and there are no catastrophes,
just special effects.

Chicago, Most Feminine of Cities

Chicago,
> big-bosomed, friendly mother of a city,
> you are of the earth.

> Of all the urban areas of the world,
> you are the most feminine.

> You don't punch, you embrace;
> You don't compete, you join;
> You nurture
> as best you can.

> Your speech is immediate;
> Not pretentious, honest.
> "Da city," "fo'ks," "by your house;"
> Words, not the King's English,
> but the singer's lullaby, the teen's "you know,"
> the teacher's lesson, the Beaneater poet's words,
> the cook's measured "pinch a dis", the mother's counsel
> and the lover's direct pronouns and verb
> in "I love you."

Your rosey cheeks say:
> "We have had the rashes of summer
> and the frost-bite from Lake Michigan."

Your soul, speaking through a light in your eyes, says:
> "We have known the joys, the hopes of springtime
> and the lingering love of fall."

Chicago is beautiful to us Chicagoans,
     as is a mother to her child;
     sweet-smelling of soap rather than of perfume;
     warm, as only she can be
     who has put tiny frozen hands in her armpits;
     gentle as only a female creator can be
     with a newborn child or a brokenhearted adult one.

Chicago is a woman, vigorous and determined,
     who labors in the home, in the office and elsewhere;
     cooking,
     scrubbing floors,
     painting,
     inventing,
     cross-guarding,
     thinking,
     nursing,
     writing insurance policies,
     shipping packages
     and running the operation.

We Chicago sports fans don't know
     how to think about the fact
     that we are a feminine city
     with vines on the walls of a stadium
     where a team is loved
     when it loses;
     how to react
     that our basketball players,
     Horace Grant and Michael Jordan,

told a man in the White House
that winning wasn't everything.

Our city is feminine
    because she is at the heart of America
    and embraces the rest of it.

    Chicago cares more, a lot more,
    and people know that;

    Chicago sings more, much more;
    and better, a lot better;
        Jazz,
        Gospel,
        Blues,
        Chicago Symphony Orchestra Chorus,
        Lyric Opera,
        Grant Park,
        and the Old Town School of Folk Music.

Our city was wild once,
    but as a young woman who wants
    to be free and to be her own self
    can be boisterous and rowdy;
    you know she remembers it
    when she sighs and when she sings.
Chicago was a tart once,
    a painted woman beneath a streetlight;
    but she wanted to be more, much more,
    and she became more, a mother.

Our city is a woman because of:
>Jane Addams, especially because of Jane Addams,
>Ida B. Wells, crusader for justice,
>Kate O'Leary, poor abused Kate,
>Bertha Palmer, motherly matron of Chicago society,
>the Everleigh sisters, Minna & Ada, even them,
>all the women of Hull House;
>wow, what they did to mother a city!
>Mother St. Frances Cabrini,
>who built hospitals and orphanages,
>and who was canonized by the church;
>Ella Flagg Young, who loved children,
>and lead the public schools;
>Harriet Monroe,
>who gave us Poetry: A Magazine of Verse;
>Edna Ferber and Margaret Ayer Barnes,
>who won us Pulitzer Prizes in literature.
>Gwendolyn Brooks, who etches in words;
>Sally Rand and Little Egypt,
>who were originals;
>Colleen Moore,
>who acted in flicks and gave us a doll house;
>Mary Garden, who sang and operated opera;
>Bessie Louise Pierce, who wrote history;
>and Sophonisba B. Breckinridge, who did sociology;
>Willye White, who could run with the wind;
>Elizabeth Wood, taking on 50 men on the City Council
>to create decent, honest, integrated
>public housing.

Jane Byrne, who was mayor;
Sen. Carol Moseley-Braun
and those who voted for her.

But more than these,
 the Native American women
 even before our history;
 pioneers;
 the Yankee school marms;
 the immigrants;
 those who died in childbirth;
 the scrub women;
 the mothers-too-soon,
 without food to eat or milk to give;
 the belles of the ball
 and those, all those, who dream.

You, as much as
 the architects,
 grain dealers,
 track layers,
 map-makers and merchants

 have made Chicago
 a city of flesh rather than steel;
 of music more than mayhem
 of milk easier than money;
 of mystery and magic;

But also,

    a sometimes beaten woman

    who can also be violent;

    who can watch her lover stomp her child;

    who can let her schools not teach;

    who can let children not find jobs;

Chicago, she's a woman,

    who, left alone, has sometimes misplaced

    her family's future,

    unsure there ever was one.

Remember, (and she doesn't believe in excuses)

    she saw her children uprooted,

    snookered in a treaty of their land;

    a wagon load of her kids scalped;

    her little ones die in her arms

        of cholera,

        diphtheria,

        rheumatic fever,

        whooping cough,

        polio,

        rickets,

        malnutrition,

        cancer

        and AIDS.

She became,

    Mary Thompson, doctor

    and teacher of women doctors;

    Julia Foster Porter, founder

of Children's Memorial Hospital;
and many women, unnamed givers
of billions of hours of hospital service;
Jessie Binford, who headed
the Juvenile Protective Association;
Alice Hamilton, doctor,
who helped unpoison the workplace;
Mary McDowell, who rowed up Bubbly Creek,
to convince the federal government to unpollute it;
and Mary Herrick, who believed
children should be educated not for jobs but for life.

Chicago,

    big-bosomed, friendly mother of a city,
you can hurt and be hurt,
you have faults and flaws,
    faith
    and much, much femininity.

    Know thyself.

The Miami Message

Rev. Mr. Kidd,
a deacon in Miami,
found a wallet,
worn, stuffed with photographs,
                holy pictures,
                four dollars
                and a Green Card.
The owner, Jose Garcia,
sad to say,
had his address changed.
A most conscientious man,
Rev. Mr. Kidd,
he sought to get word to Jose Garcia.
He looked in the Greater Miami phone directory.
Muchos Jose Garcias there,
pero, no.
A persistent man,
the deacon advertised
in the Miami Herald.
Pero no, pero no, mi amigo.
The deacon, relentless he was,
asked the church's janitor,
who was Cuban,
to let out the word
on the streetcorners of LaCalle Ocho.
Pero si, pero si.
And that is how
the message got to Garcia
in 1993.

ACROSS
AMERICA

Fishing Stories in Kentucky

Never caught his name;
nor he, mine.
It wasn't necessary.
We were
two men
sitting on adjoining porch swings
in Grand Rivers,
Kentucky
in front of the Iron Kettle,
where they serve down-home cooking.
We were talking fishing.
He had already told me
how many of which fish
he had caught this trip,
and how many years
he had been fishing,
what the weather had been like
these last two weeks
and which fish
he liked best to eat .
And they would be
blue gills.
And he had laughed
out of embarrassment
because a true fisherman
isn't supposed
to like fish

OUR DINOSAURS ARE DYING

you can catch
with a worm, a hook and a line.
The main subject
fishermen
want to talk about
was yet to come up:
pollution.
In Canada,
he said,
he had fished
in a wilderness lake.
It was later
he learned that
a nearby uranium mine
had loaded it
with large doses of mercury.
"Who knows
what else
them fish had?"
he pondered.
Part of the Ohio River
up by Louisville,
he noted,
had been closed to fishermen.
"Benzine in the water,"
he complained.
"Awful stuff."

He swung back and forward
on the porch,
then paused.
"Used to fish
up near Ludington, Mich.
with my brother,"
he said.
"Did it for 30 years.
The fish started getting worms
and we never went back."
He paused and swung again.
"Around here,"
he said,
"the waters seem
to be getting cleaner.
The government
gets after them polluters."
Fish stories are different
these days, I thought.
I nodded to him,
then swung back and a little forward.

The West According to
Georgia O'Keeffe

Georgia O'Keeffe,
no matter
what people say,
did not invent
the bright, bright colors
of the Western skies.
They are there yet.
Nor did she create
the ochers and reds
of the New Mexico and Arizona rocks.
They are still on fire
with those hues.
She just copied them
in oils
and brought them east.

Niagara Falls

At Niagara Falls,
kids are tempted
to go over
in a barrel
or at least to cross
on a tightrope,
a challenge
to their courage, imagination and limits.
They are not allowed to do either.
Commercializers,
knowing this,
have saturated the area
with bumper cars,
ferris wheels
and 100 other rides.
C'mon.
If you can't sell drugs
near a school,
you shouldn't be allowed
to have an amusement park
near a natural wonder.

Logging

60 years ago;
they worked this mountain
in Smokey Mountain National Park,
logger teams of three did.
Each had:
a lead chipper and its two sawyers.
Replaceable as a two-handed saw,
each drove itself
to earn a few dollars
fell one more tree
and meet its quota.
A park brochure
remembers
today
the long-gone forests
and
the exploited sawyers and lead chippers,
who also came and went.

The Old Ways of the Amish

The Amish,
gentle folk
with quaint costumes,
bearded men
and "old ways,"
are close to the earth
and to their God.
Harlan is a dairy farmer
and thankful
he grew up in their way,
on their path.
He has close family,
cousins and other relatives
all over
the heart of America,
farmers mostly, like him,
but not all.
"Our people,
I think,
move more often
than your people do,"
he says.
He produces milk
for the marketplace.
"A very good quality,"
he assures us.
It's pasteurized,
has to be.
Milk that the Amish drink

is not,
because of the old ways.
The various groups in Iowa,
                        Indiana,
                        Ohio,
                        Illinois,
                        Kentucky,
                        and Pennsylvania
have different old ways.
Some Amish
have tractors
and cars,
others use animals
and horse-drawn carriages.
A few,
very few,
are organic farmers,
ones who don't use
chemical fertilizers.
Most,
Harlan says,
have become too big,
too successful
to go back
to that old way.
And they include,
he says,
ones who still
use horses and mules.

The Rock Climber

Heights terrify him,
he tells me,
but still he rock climbs,
straight up the face
of cliffs
with a rope,
using fingerholds a quarter-inch deep,
following routes
and clipping carabeeners;
simple, yes, for a monkey
but not for you or me.
Wait a minute,
didn't he say he was afraid?
Yes, scared even to look down.
Yet, he climbs:

        The Gunks in New York,
        Devil's Tower in Wyoming,
        Devil's Lake in Wisconsin,
        Joshua Tree in California,
        simulated walls in gyms,
        retaining walls in the city,
        along the lake and the highways.

"Easy," he says.
"I don't look down...very often."
And the rest of us,
we don't understand...at all,
unless it's that
life isn't as scary, I guess,
for those who go through it
just looking up.

The New American Nomad

The new American nomad,
she.
150,000 miles
on her fifth wheel trailer and pickup truck;
her home,
her only one,
travelling
from coast to coast.
A widow,
no children,
69, retired,
alone.
And, yet,
not alone.
There are others
such as she.
"Women RVing,"
they call themselves.
She
and other, older women
travelling
across the country
all year
alone.
"Escapees,"
is a name they use.
They travel
from Florida to California,
where it stays warm
and where campers and trailers

don't rust.
The new American nomads,
they,
driven to escape
the boredom
that is often
the price and cost
of being an older woman alone.
Rediscovering America,
these women,
its South
and especially its West,
visiting Indian ruins,
attending pow wows and festivals.
Meeting people, this woman,
she travels
in her fifth wheel and pickup,
stopping
in Coast to Coast campgrounds
where her membership
allows her to stay
at $1 a night
but only for 7 days;
then, marching on,
sometimes visiting
relatives and old friends,
but mainly moving on, cheaply, freely;
escaping
the limitations
of boredom and too little money;

staying in a campground
in Las Vegas,
not gambling,
but enjoying the freebies
given to encourage people
to come and gamble.
In California,
she picks raisins off the vines
after the grape-workers
have been through;
getting them for free,
the dried ones
left behind;
doing it with another woman,
also a nomad,
a once-a-year friend.
Where next,
this nomad?
No, not there,
nor there;
but out there,
West,
where people seem friendlier
and the relics have been left behind
by earlier
American nomads.
What ruin or relic
will mark her trail?
A worn-out fifth wheel or truck?
Herself a grape

that is not becoming a raisin,
she has found
a way to escape,
or,
at least,
to delay the process
of drying on the vine,
this new American nomad.

Strider on the Appalachian Trail

"Strider,"
was the trail name
he took
when first he set out
on the Appalachian Trail.
291 pounds
was his weight
46 days ago,
when he started
on Springer Mountain
in Georgia.
He was striding along
the 2,000 mile, mountain-top trail
headed
toward Maine and Mount Katadhin there.
Strider,
when he started,
was big
and he was inexperienced.
Then, if he looked down,
he could see the valleys,
but not his toes.
Never before had he hiked
even a ways.
But he had sold his carpet business
and had begun.
At 291 pounds,
he was slower than most.
They walked with him for a while,
and then moved on.

Some,
who started with him,
had quit at the first resupply depot.
He went on.
It was physical,
at first.
"Oh, was it ever!"
he said.
And then, it got mental,
very mental.
It was not work,
it was not play.
This aloneness in life,
even though you met others!
This not seeing a person you knew!
He walks
and he walks
and he walks
in nature's sanctuary
amid plants
which stay and blossom
behind him.
He carries
with him
a special handpump,
to purify the water,
along the route.
He eats trail food
and stays in campsites
and primitive shelters,

continuing on
with a backpack
that weighs 60 pounds,
replenishing his food
every five or six days,
moving on
not only on the trail
but in life.
It is the end of May,
a month and a half along,
and he is passing
from Tennessee to North Carolina.
He wears a turkey buzzard feather
in his slouched hat
and his clothes fit loose.
He can see his toes now,
very easily,
thank you.
He has lost six to eight inches
off his belt,
almost a pound a day.
Strider is down
to 250 pounds now.
"No McDonald's or 7-11's on this trail,"
he explains.
He has his staff
and he strides off,
smiling
about two apples
someone just gave him.

Before Us

Before you
and before me,
where we live
and where we play,
did paleo-indians
with fear and bravery
there pursue and hunt
some frightening, 14-foot,
long-tusked,
elephant-skinned
mastodon or wooly mammoth?

. . .

On our street,
on our lot,
did their descendents
change man's survival odds
by inventing the atlatl,
a slingshot-like thong,
to help them whirl and throw
straighter and stronger
than ever before
their well-aimed spears?

. . .

By your river,
over there near your stream,
did those people

we awkwardly label
middle archaic
first carve hooks
from bones
to catch fish
5,000 years ago,
returning, settling on the site
again next year
when the fishing had been good?

      • • •

Over paths now your roads,
down the one become your street,
did those who built mounds
in 1,000 B. C.
also travel to trade
beads, rings and pendants
for shells and conches
and exchange food for food,
giving up their nomads ways,
to become hunters, farmers and traders?

      • • •

Next to your park,
in a neighboring forest,
did a people
in the time of Christ,
settle their village

and bury their dead
with axes and spears
newly-fashioned
for an afterlife?

          • • •

Along paths now your railroad tracks,
and over routes become your interstates,
did those we call
the Late Woodland people
during Europe's Dark Ages
travel and return home
with alligator teeth
and grizzly bear bones
and, with skill and art,
craft tools and jewelry?

          • • •

To your town,
into your neighborhood,
did Cahokians come
from along the Mississippi
with fresh prosperity and a culture
born of urbanization
and a new strain of corn
and develop a new era
as Europe survived its Middle Ages,
its wars and its pestilence?

Where you work,
and where you worship,
did there reside
a content and rich population
that believed they were the most favored,
the most powerful,
most god-protected people
in the world?

. . .

Before you and before me,
even before history,
were there peoples
who didn't comprehend
any better than we
who they were
and what it is all about?

To My Friends

When I was four years,
I lost my best pal,
a cowboy doll
with holsters.
For years,
I was sure
I would never get him back.
I have,
in good friends.

PEOPLE

An Alley Picker

Gino Tenuta,
recycler of the past,
frequenter of alleys,
garbage picker,
if you will,
but a rescuer from dumpsters
of things still useful:
records,
books,
pictures,
radios,
clothes,
furniture
and an occasional toy.
Too nervous
to hold a job,
he was put out on the street
himself,
many times.
He survived
anyhow
and stayed
happy and loving,
the last authentic Hippie.
You never buckled under,
buddy.

OUR DINOSAURS ARE DYING

Helen Keller

Helen Keller
couldn't see them
but she could touch the stars,
reaching them
on beams
of fierce personal freedom,
    common sense perspective
    and unshakable tolerance,
materials often invisible
to the human eye.

Walt Whitman

Walt Whitman was a poet
for a long, long time
before anyone cared.
"I hear America singing, the varied carols,"
he wrote
in Leaves of Grass.
In the Civil War,
        he was a comforter and consoler
of dying soldiers,
who neither knew nor cared
he was gay.

Willie

Willie didn't have much going for him,
not much at all.
No job and no prospects;
Poorly educated
and barely able to read;
feared and unwanted,
and he couldn't tell you why.
Was he being open with me
or just jiving?
Either way, here's what he said:
"When I walks down the sidewalk,
and I sees two people holdin' hands,
I walks between 'em.
Once, I stopped and asked for a light.
The guy started to give me one
and I went and hit 'im."
Why?
"I dunno."

The Legend of Al Capone

Al Capone,
researchers know,
was not
as powerful,
as mean,
nor even as interesting
as history or rather, legend,
has painted him.
Certainly,
the man with the facial scar
was not as rich
as the Guinness Book of Records
claimed for him.
So who was he, what was he?
A legend
taller than any building
in the Loop
and a man
whose name and message
reached the most distant spots
in either hemisphere.
"Ratatat...Al Capone,"
they will tell you
in Timbuktu
and Tierra del Fuego,
in Chile,
Greenland
and the Outback.
Little kids
and very old men

will smile and say his name
when you say, "Chicago."
Why was this man
so extraordinarily infamous?
Two reasons:
the machine gun
and no convictions for murder
for himself or his mob.
That double message
laid out the possibility,
the means,
of instant, absolute retaliation
and of getting away with it.
The name of Al Capone
swept around the globe
faster
than the voice of righteousness
and farther
than the arms of the law.
"Ratatat,"
it said,
retaliate now
and send a message
to your parents,
the bullies,
your boss,
the government
or the rich.
"Ratatat"

and the playing field
will be leveled.
And you can win
it all,
and get away with it,
you,
Al Capone.

The Truth About Lying

Philibert Ramstetter, O.F.M.
He was old, straight and tall
like a Cedar of Lebanon,
the kind they used up
to build
fortresses and temples,
homes that lasted forever
and ships that weathered
many storms.
He was a Franciscan
and a teacher of philosophy,
an awesome man,
noted by many
for his intellect
and by others
for his caring.
He stood like the tallest tree
when he said it.
Although he whispered them,
the words seemed
to thunder down
and shake the desks before him.
"A lie,"
he told
the seminarians
in front of him,
"is a violation of the intellect."
A Cedar of Lebanon uttered
that truth about not telling the truth.

Collaborators

A blind photographer:
a contradiction in terms,
you say.
How can it be?
The mind and heart
have their ways,
however,
and so did Russell Ogg,
who had photographed
all the top movie stars
but now was a blind
photographer
of hummingbirds.
Well,
he wasn't exactly
the picture taker.
The birds were.
He had
the tiny,
iridescent
visitors
to his patio
take their own
pictures
when they fluttered
past the lens
of his "seeing eye" camera
in order to drink
from a feeder
he had set out.

And thus,
photos were taken
that have appeared
in books,
calendars
and art galleries,
the works
of two collaborators:
a blind man and a hummingbird.

A One-Woman Crusade

Bubbly Creek,
in days gone by,
an awful, stinking, putrid
branch of the Chicago River.
Bubbly Creek,
fetid sewer for the stockyards,
about which tales, tall tales, were told
of large, slimy, sickening
bubbles breaking a crusted surface
to engulf man and beast.
Bubbly Creek,
which polluted the river and the air
with the unimaginable
and the insufferable.
Who would do battle
and when?
1870, 1880, 1890,
1900, 1910, 1920?
The creek bubbled and perked
with a slime made
of the hair, fat and offal
of long-dead animals.
Meatpacker Gustavus Swift,
who made a profit
on everything from the pig
except its squeal,
complained
that Bubbly Creek
was a proof of waste
by his employees

and therefore a loss of his profits.
He would not do battle,
he would not clean it up.
But Mary McDowell,
anointed friend and disciple
of Jane Addams,
she would.
She begged,
pleaded,
argued,
strategized
and persisted
to get those in power
to do something.
They didn't.
So she rowed a rowboat
up Bubbly Creek
and thereby proved
it was a navigable stream
subject
to federal regulation.
She won.
And Bubbly Creek
today
is a hidden place in Chicago
where birds sing along the banks,
an occasional fish jumps
and no bubbles come up
to get you.

An American Beauty

We humans,
since voice
first uttered metaphor,
have attempted to pay homage
to a rose
and to share
its discovery and experience
with others of our species.
It is given
to each of us
to have done this,
to speak
of its fragrance,
       its sensuous texture
      and its deep hues.
It surprises us
with its incomparable color,
      form,
      majesty,
      uniqueness,
      and aroma.
We imitate the rose
in carvings,
      glass etchings,
      paintings,
      perfumes
      and paragraphs.

We use it to honor
                    our graduates,
                    our performers,
                    our brides,
                    our mothers
                    and our dead.
We propagate,
crossbreed
and protect it,
plotting gardens
and building trellises for it.
We grow,
buy
and sell them,
giving them away,
a dozen at a time,
with long stems
and short ones.
We know the prick
of their protective barbs.
To our species,
a rose is synonymous
with fragile,
fragrant
and mysterious beauty.
Our praise for it,
however,
wilts even faster
than the delicate
white,

yellow,
pink
or deep red petals.
Only the words
of Gertrude Stein
survive
because
she avoided
comparison, adjective, metaphor
and verbiage
other than reminding us
a rose is a rose is a rose.
Oh, yes!

The Forgotten "Coloreds"

Forgotten
are
the symbols,
the acts,
the conditions,
the limitations
and the facts of life
that African-Americans
faced
in the North
little more than a generation ago.
Included on the list:
the "colored" balconies
of movie theaters;
the hospital wards for Negroes
in the ones that admitted them;
the "members only" restrictions
of swimming pools
with membership
costing a quarter for whites
but not available
to anyone else;
the restrictive covenants
covering subdivisions and whole neighborhoods;
the separate and unequal schools;
the Negro sections of cemeteries,
the few which did accept all;
the word "white"
in employment ads;
the powerful

union hiring hall exclusion practices;
the golf course,
amusement park,
campground
and public beach
no admittance policies;
the redlining
by insurance companies;
the "need not apply" regulations
for taxicab,
banking,
conductor,
retail store,
office worker
and executive job and positions;
the "We don't serve coloreds"
at restaurants,
bars
and hotels;
the "I'm sorry, but it's not up to me"
all the time over the telephone;
the "We think
you'd be happier
with your own"
at prayer meetings,
revivals
and churches;
the "Sorry,
but you don't qualify" answer
from banks or savings and loans;

the "You were speeding, boy"
of the traffic cop;
the injustice
of the justice system;
the distance
of the social worker
and the disdain
of the socially prominent volunteer;
the bricks through the window
when you tried
to move out of the "Black Belt;"
the righteousness,
the patronizing,
the racist jokes;
the sexual innuendos
of so many,
so often;
the indignity
of seeing one's children
ignored by teachers,
and picked on by other students;
the frustration,
the hurt,
yes,
and even the acceptance
of it all.
Forgotten!
Why?

Women and American History

"History of Our Country,"
a high school textbook,
copyright 1929,
a leaf of Americana
had floated down the stream
and sunk in the sea of usage.
This copy, an exception,
old and threadbare,
mine for a dollar
at a fleamarket.
"A bargain,"
the lady had said.
On the cover,
images of the Santa Maria
and an aeroplane.
I wanted this book
snatched back from the sea
to learn how much
some things had changed
while other
stayed the way they were.
This book contains
no such words as:
Depression,
World War II,
television,
atomic energy,
space technology,
Civil Rights,

computers
or,
of course,
virtual reality.
Women,
they were mentioned,
but very few by name.
There were
even two shorts section
on them,
but the index told all.
It named
331 men,
but only 11 women.
Written
on the front and back flaps
of the books were the dates
in the 1930s
when students
thought
they were studying
the panorama of
American history.

A Young Lady

I know a young lady
who
at least once a season
goes to the amusement park.
She rides every rollercoaster
and tries
every new ride.
She has been doing it
for more than 50 years.

What Love Is

Love is not what they say it is.
Everyone tells me that
and so do I.

Unknown Soldiers

No military guard,
no eternal flame,
no unknown soldier ceremony
at the Civil War cemetery
at Fort Donelson in Tennessee.
In rows it has the graves
of 655 Union soldiers,
fallen taking the fort in 1862.
Of them,
504 lie in the ground
unknown and unidentified.
A special sadness
hangs over this cemetery,
a remembering of families,
                    wives,
                    mothers,
                    fathers,
                    children
                    and friends
who never knew
exactly where
or for certain
loved ones died.
And, yet,
on the day in 1862,
when the North learned
whatever there was to learn,
church bells rang
and the people danced in the streets.
Union forces,

hallelujah,
had won their first victory
in the war between the states,
the one between brothers.
The bells up North
no longer can be heard,
but the sadness hangs still
over the cemetery
where comrades,
too shocked and too inexperienced
to stop and identify them,
had buried their dead.

The Tall Grass Prairie

The tall grass prairie
which once served
as the dinner table
for thousands of species
of birds,
            insects
            and animals,
was not one for man.
The pioneers cut its sward,
therefore,
to grow his corn,
            wheat
            and barley
to build his homes,
            construct train tracks and roads
            and put up factories.
The tall grass prairies were,
to the human eye,
vast patches,
swaying in the breeze,
rich in bright, bursting colors,
grasses and flowers.
The earth used them
to proclaim its abundance
and even man
called them beautiful,
as he destroyed them.
But, surprise, surprise!
Whenever the fields
are left fallow;

the railroad tracks,
torn up;
farm houses,
abandoned
and factories,
closed;
the tall grass prairie
comes back,
offering a dinner table
for thousands of species
and a celebrated quilt for one.

WORDS

A Piece of Immortality

"A book
is a piece of immortality."
Is that metaphor
or reality?
Can we touch the past
through a tome
and can the future
reach us by means of one.
Metaphorically yes
and, yes, in reality.
Some day,
someone
will read this book
and hear my voice
though I be dead.
I hope that person
will smile
and say one word,
"Yes."
I hear it now.
You can say it
even though I'm not dead.
I hear that, too.

How to Make a Buck
by Reading my Poetry

We poets,
at least some of us,
would really
like to sell our poems;
which means
have you buy them.
What we need,
I'm told,
is a marketing plan,
a solid-theme
advertising campaign
that will get you
and keep you;
or,
preferably,
addict you.
We'd like the money spent
on our poems
to come from your entertainment budget,
what you lay out
for drinks or cigarettes.
How about that?
Our poems are a lot better
for you
than they are
and the long-term cost
especially
is a lot less.

Some who don't need
as much food as they eat
could use that budget
to buy my poems.
My poetry
should want
you to be a better person,
so maybe its cost
could be looked upon
as a minor "sin tax."
Subsidies,
that what you need.
The government
should help you pay for it.
I know what.
We'll print
only so many copies
of my books
and then
they will go up in value
as you hold onto them.
"Buy my poems
and make money,"
that will be the selling slogan.
Now,
we all know
poets are supposed
to be above the crass ways
of medicine shows,
two-bit reformers

and politicians.
Still,
we poets,
at least some of us,
would really
like to sell our poems.
Ever hear of a poetry auction?

How to Write a Poem

You walk through a field,
smell the flowers
and then, unhumbly,
try to recreate it,
having to share
whether you want to or not.

Why Write?

If I were alone,
all by myself on an island
forever
and had not pen and paper
nor usable arms;
I would go
to where the wind did not blow,
perhaps, a cave,
if it were there;
and I would walk
upward toward a higher place
and leave behind my footprints.
But it would be all right
if I walked in the opposite direction,
if
I were so inclined.

Where to Sell Poetry?

Poetry writers
ask, "Where can I sell a poem?"
The answer I've heard is,
"The same place
where you buy one."
And that answer is poetic
justice,
don't you think?

Ah, Platonic Love!

We have to be careful
of letting teenagers read the work
of the great philosophers.
Did you know
that Plato proposed
communal mating,
free love
and mixed gymnastics
for boys and girls
clad only in their virtue?
We can't have young people
reading about that.
Don't let them
see this poem, either.

Written on a Monday Morning

Monday mornings
are not hard
like

       death,

       taxes

       or time in prison.

I try
to remember that.

Babies

Fledglings,
kittens,
puppies,
chicks,
bunnies,
cubs,
lambs,
foals,
kids,
owlets,
calves,
joeys,
and babies:
without them,
there would be no tomorrow
nor one to cuddle today.

The Real Age of Dinosaurs

They say the dinosaurs
lived
100,000 million years ago,
give or take some;
back in the

        Triassic,

        Jurassic

        and Cretaceous periods.
100,000 million year ago?
No.
They were alive
when we were four or five.
We all remember.

Ads

A TV ad,
like a pebble
found on the beach,
can be full of fascination
for five or ten seconds.
Then,
it's time
to throw it
back in the water,
don't you think?

The Elements

Water, wind, earth and fire.
Is that all there is?
My experience says so.
Religion and science say, "No."
But, then they don't believe
that experience is everything.
That, you see, is their trick.
Think about it.

Responsibility, as in Personal

When the word,
"personal,"
is put
in front of
"responsibility,"
a good,
strong,
healthy
word,
it becomes pregnant,
the bearer of our meaning,
of our purpose.

The Greatest Argument Ever

"It was a new Chevrolet,"
he said adamantly.
"No, it was last year's Pontiac,"
the young man
on the bench next to him argued.
"You could tell,"
he asserted
to buttress his argument.
"You are both wrong,"
a third said.
Each repeated himself
for the next 15 minutes.
Then, the bell rang,
calling the three
young, cloistered novices
away from the park,
behind the slatted fence
along the other side of which
a car had passed
for a second.
Aren't very many
arguments
just like that—
stupid
beyond belief?

Did Anyone Ever Tell You This Before?

Get lost in a book.
It's a wonderful place
to find yourself.

Definitions

Poetry,
not dictionaries
should define words.
All right, let the dictionaries
spell them,
but not be allowed to let them shrivel
like plums in the sun
on their way
to prunedom.

No Wonder They are Called Stoics

God love the stoics,
even if the early Christians
did destroy
every one of their works
because they were human-centered.

The Red Wolf

How would you
like to have
a coyote in your past?
That's what's facing
the red wolf,
a funny animal to be.
Down to 200
were he and she
when man
decided to breed them
in captivity.
Their cousin,
the coyote
had already had his own program,
which meant
having his way with them,
and doing what came naturally.
The red wolves, we now see,
didn't become almost extinct.
They only lost
their identity.

Just Talkin'

Slang, streettalk, jive and rap:
languages of the people,
real ones, you know.
Damn it
how can we ban and restrict them
or, even worse,
allow teachers and schools to do so?
Maybe, cuz
sometimes they be more expressive
than the man's English.
And, then, again
it could be
the man's culture
'posed on, not created by,
the folks
that the man
with mo' money thinks
he be better than.

Get Old Anyway

"He's important,"
they used to say.
Now,
he's elderly
and they don't say it
anymore.
What do they know?
His vote
is still there
for the politician;
his soul,
for the priest;
his health,
or lack of it,
for the doctor;
his wealth,
for the descendants.
All he wants
is a little respect
and that
is all he gets.
Get old anyway.

What Should He Do?

What should he do?
A friend
has done a heinous thing.
Tears come
but not answers.
This is true,
inconsolable sadness.

The Ultimate Weapon of Columbus, GA

Columbus, Georigia.
That's where ˙
they spent the Civil War
building the ultimate weapon.
It was a powerful gunboat;
no, more than that.
It was an ironclad,
a ram,
a winner for the losing side.
On the Chattahoochee River,
in 1862,
they started
to construct this monster ship;
one, they were confident,
could end the North's blockade,
destroy its river gunboats,
sink its transport ships
and the mighty Yankee rams as well.
This weapon-building
gave hope and purpose
for more than three years
galvanizing the city of Columbus.
This mammoth boat
with skin of iron
was to become
an awful,
dreadful,
life-taking
weapon
that would blast away

at ships and forts
alike.
The C.S.S. Jackson,,
they were calling it.
The ram's chief officer
would be a captain
no less
than William Watts Carnes,
the man who had commanded
the first ironclad,
the Virginia,
also known
as the Merrimac,
the weapon
that had frightened
 old Abe Lincoln
himself.
That ship
alone
came close
to wiping out the Northern fleet;
would have, too,
except for bad luck
and the last minute appearance
of the North's first ironclad,
the Monitor.
Once again,
the brave,
bright
and brilliant

captain,
the cream of Southern sailing men,
would have a ship,
a more magnificent ship,
by far,
under his feet.
Destiny would crown
his forehead.
The building went slow.
Iron became hard to come by,
very hard.
Even wood was scarce
and so were able workers,
many taken for the army.
The effort
ground determinedly onward.
1862 was gone.
as the Southern armies won
and its navy lost.
1863 passed
with Vicksburg and Gettysburg,
terrible losses;
1864 saw
graves across the South
and Atlanta lost to Sherman's army.
1865 came
and the South held on.
The ram was ready at last
and the desperate South
had forgotten its ultimate weapon,

but the people of Columbus had not.
Proudly and hopefully,
they launched their ram
into the waters
of the Chattahoochee.
It crunched
hard on the bottom, the C.S.S. Jackson did:
too heavy
and the river too shallow.
The Yankees came to Columbus
victors over the South.
They buried the ship
in the river
so it could never be used
should the South rise again.
Over the years,
it remained
a Civil War
anecdote,
a footnote,
a sad little tale.
Then, in 1964,
some 99 years later,
the fearsome, ultimate weapon
was dredged up from its grave
to be put on display
to attract visitors
and show them,
including the Yankee ones,
what they might have had to face.

High Rises vs. Skyscrapers

Skyscrapers,
did they really
scrape the sky?
Nah.
That's why they don't
call them that anymore.
High rises,
that's modern language for you.
They do rise high;
now, that's true.
They're a commodity, not poetry;
so, you have to guess,
the change had to do with
truth in packaging.

Peace

Peace
cannot exist
between
the mouse and the eagle,
nor between
brothers and sisters
who are not equal.

The Small Businessman

His business he opened,
having read
a stack of brochures,
two of pamphlets,
three books
and one pack of promotional materials.
He, of course,
took night classes
and two seminars;
carefully listened
to his big-deal brother-in-law
and arranged and rearranged his stock
12 times.
Still, his business
did not do well,
not well at all.
Then,
one day,
he put himself across the counter
and looked back
as a customer would.
Eureka!
Promptly,
he lowered his prices,
learned to say "yes,"
began answering every question
as honestly as he could
and starting smiling a real smile.
Oh, yes,
he is doing much better now.

FINAL
THOUGHTS

The Holocaust Remembered

Phyllis is Jewish.
That is why,
she said,
she is pleased
her friends have
a secret hiding place
under the stairs
in their basement,
even though she knows,
almost all of their friends
would be targeted
for one reason or another,
and so would they.

Guns

Hate guns
not
because they are evil,
but because they are dangerous.
Don't just stand there,
do something.

Her Obituary

Her life was everything she ever felt.
Do not try to convince her
it was anything different
for she is dead.
Think of that as you look in the casket.
Nothing she ever experienced is there.
No passion,
no love,
no anger,
no hate.
no need,
no hope.
Something happened,
and she took that with her too.

The Darndest Things

Kids say
the most awful things
and the most wonderful,
sometimes
at the same time.
And we adults who think
we always
know the difference
turn into monitors and censors.
What a mistake!

The Game of Life

If I were a general,
I would outflank them.
If I were a target,
I would turn sideways.
If I were the enemy,
I would try not to be.
If I lost, I would ask why aren't they giving me the cup?
There are strategies,
That not even Napoleon knew about.
There are games to be played
and our lives to be lived
and we decide what winning is.
You bet we do,
but then don't bet me.
I win.